NICHE MASTERY

NICHE MASTERY

NICHE MASTERY

A Blueprint for Online Entrepreneurs to Discover, Dominate and Build a Profitable Thriving Brand in 60 Minutes

By

Coulter J. Weldon

Copyright © by **Coulter J. Weldon** 2024. All rights reserved.

Before this document is duplicated or reproduced in any manner, the publisher's consent must be gained. Therefore, the contents within can neither be stored electronically, transferred, nor kept in a database. Neither in Part nor full can the document be copied, scanned, faxed, or retained without approval from the publisher or creator.

TABLE OF CONTENTS

INTRODUCTION   **11**
THE NICHE CONUNDRUM   **11**
    Why Finding Your Niche Stalls Online Success   11
    The Myth of the "Perfect Passion": Unveiling Hidden Profit Potential   14
    Analysis Paralysis Prison: Why You're Stuck and How to Escape with Action   17

PART 1: THE NICHE MASTERY FRAMEWORK - A DEEP DIVE   **21**
CHAPTER 1   **21**
DEMYSTIFYING THE NICHE MASTERY: UNDERSTANDING BECKLER'S CORE CONCEPTS 21
    Inexperience as an Asset: How a Beginner's Mindset Fuels Niche Discovery   21
    The Three Pillars of a Profitable Niche: Passion, Profit, and Audience   24

CHAPTER 2:   **29**
THE PROFIT POTENTIAL FORMULA: DECODING NICHE PROFITABILITY   **29**
    Breaking Down the Formula: Demand, Competition, and Affiliate Programs   29
    Worksheets & Templates: Putting the Formula into Action   33

CHAPTER 3:   **39**
BEYOND THE BOOK: UNVEILING HIDDEN NICHES 39
    Exploring Untapped Markets: Strategies for

Identifying Niche Opportunities   39

Case Studies & Reader Success Stories:
Real-World Examples of Niche Mastery Triumphs   43

PART 2: VALIDATING YOUR NICHE - FROM SPARK TO CERTAINTY   49
CHAPTER 4:   49
ACTIONABLE VALIDATION TECHNIQUES: MOVING BEYOND THE ONE-HOUR MARK   49

Competitor Analysis: Understanding the Landscape and Identifying Gaps   49

Beyond the Google Search: Unmasking Your Ideal Audience   53

From Data to Narrative: The Power of Storytelling and Community Building   58

Understanding Keyword Research: 62

Engaging with Online Communities: Validating Niche Ideas Through Interaction   67

CHAPTER 5:   73
OVERCOMING NICHE SELECTION ROADBLOCKS: MINDSET SHIFTS AND SOLUTIONS   73

Taming the Fear of Failure: Embracing Experimentation in Niche Selection   73

Imposter Syndrome and the "Shiny Object Syndrome": Strategies to Stay Focused   77

What if My Niche is Too Small? The Power of Micro-Niches in a Saturated Market   81

PART 3: BUILDING YOUR ONLINE BUSINESS - BONUS CHAPTER   85
CHAPTER 6:   85

FROM NICHE TO EMPIRE: THE INITIAL STEPS OF BUILDING YOUR ONLINE BUSINESS — 85

- Choosing a Business Model: Affiliate Marketing, E-commerce, or Beyond? — 85
- Crafting Your Brand Identity: Standing Out in a Crowded Marketplace — 88
- Content Creation Essentials: Attracting Your Target Audience with Valuable Content — 92

CHAPTER 7: — 97
LAUNCHING AND GROWING YOUR ONLINE BUSINESS: ESSENTIAL TOOLS AND STRATEGIES — 97

- Building Your Digital Home: Essential Website Creation Platforms — 97
- Spreading the Word: Effective Marketing Tactics for Online Businesses — 100
- Content is King (and Queen): Strategies to Leverage Different Formats — 101

CONCLUSION: — 104
THE NICHE MASTERY JOURNEY - A LIFELONG PURSUIT OF SUCCESS — 104

- Continuous Learning and Niche Refinement: Embracing Growth and Adaptation — 104
- Embracing Growth and Adaptation — 107
- The Power of Community - Building Networks and Sharing Your Entrepreneurial Journey — 112
- Your First Steps Towards Online Business Success — 117
- Profitable Niches for Beginners: Launching Quickly and Leveraging Your Skills — 121

NICHE MASTERY

*H*ello, and welcome to the Niche Mastery workshop. I'm Coulter J. Weldon.

Do you ever feel like you're trapped in a hamster wheel of online courses, ebooks, and endless "get rich quick" schemes, all promising a path to financial freedom that never quite appears? You spend hours researching and learning "perfect" systems, but nothing seems to stick. The dream of escaping the 9-to-5 grind feels further away than ever, replaced by a nagging sense of frustration and self-doubt.

Maybe that's you. Maybe, like me, weldon, you've poured your heart and soul into building an online business, only to be met with crickets chirping in the vast emptiness of the internet. Countless late nights spent hunched over a laptop, sifting through endless niche ideas, each one seeming more saturated than the last. The fear of picking the wrong niche, the paralysis of analysis, it all becomes a suffocating weight, pushing you further towards giving up on your dreams.

But here's the thing, Weldon (and whoever else might be feeling the same way), what if I told you there's a different way? What if there was a method that could cut through the noise and help you identify a profitable niche, one that aligns with your passions and doesn't require years of trial and error?

This book, "Niche Mastery," isn't another empty promise. It's a lifeline thrown to those drowning in a sea of "gurus" and conflicting advice. It's the story of countless individuals, just like you and me, who used this revolutionary framework to escape the online wilderness and build thriving online businesses.

This isn't a magic bullet, but it's a powerful tool that can dramatically shorten your journey to success. Consider "Niche Mastery" an investment in yourself, a chance to break free from the cycle of frustration and finally step onto a path paved with purpose and profitability. Don't waste another minute feeling lost. Let's navigate this online maze together and find your niche for success.

INTRODUCTION

THE NICHE CONUNDRUM

Why Finding Your Niche Stalls Online Success

*I*magine this: you're at a bustling food court, overwhelmed by a dizzying array of options. Burgers sizzling, sushi glistening, fragrant curries bubbling away – it's a feast for the senses, but a nightmare for a decision. Do you crave a juicy burger or a light and healthy poke bowl? Maybe the rich aroma of Thai curry is calling your name.

The problem? Indecision. You can't choose because you haven't considered your own taste and what would truly satisfy you. The online business world is a lot like that food court. Countless gurus preach the gospel of "**multiple income streams**," urging you to be everything to everyone. But here's the truth: **being a**

jack-of-all-trades online is a recipe for overwhelm and ultimately, failure.

The secret weapon every successful online entrepreneur wields is a powerful tool called a **'NICHE'**. It's not a cage, but a laser focus – a way to understand your ideal customer's deepest desires and tailor your offerings to perfectly meet them.

Here's why the "everything for everyone" approach stalls your online success:

. **The Dilution Trap:** Scattered efforts lead to mediocre content and marketing that resonates with no one deeply. You become a faceless voice in the crowd, lost in a sea of generic competitors.

. **The Passion Paradox:** Trying to appeal to everyone dilutes your passion. You lose the spark that ignites creativity and fuels your drive. When you focus on a niche you care about, genuine enthusiasm shines through, attracting the right audience.

- **The Authority Abyss:** Spreading yourself thin prevents you from becoming a true authority in any one area. Niching down allows you to develop deep expertise, making you a trusted advisor in your chosen space.

Think back to the food court. Wouldn't you rather have the perfectly seasoned pad that from the vendor specializing in Thai cuisine, rather than a mediocre burger from a place trying to be everything to everyone?

Finding your niche isn't about limitation; it's about liberation. It's about focusing your energy, expertise, and passion to create something truly remarkable for a specific audience. "Niche Mastery" is your roadmap to escaping the indecision trap and unlocking the online success you deserve. Let's ditch the buffet mentality and find your signature dish – the one that will leave your ideal customers wanting more.

The Myth of the "Perfect Passion": Unveiling Hidden Profit Potential

Ah, the "perfect passion." That elusive dream that supposedly holds the key to online business success. We spend countless hours scouring the internet, chasing after niches that spark a flicker of excitement, only to find them lacking in profitability. The result? Frustration, self-doubt, and the sinking feeling that maybe online success just isn't for us.

But here's the truth: the "perfect passion" is a myth. It's a roadblock that keeps us stuck, hindering us from uncovering the hidden profit potential that lies within. Here's why:

. **The Passion Paradox:** While passion is important, it can also blind us to opportunities. Chasing the "perfect passion" narrows our focus, preventing us from exploring niches that might not ignite a spark at first glance, but hold immense potential for growth and profit.

. **The "Unicorn" Niche:** The "perfect passion" often leads us on a wild goose chase for non-existent unicorn niches - areas that are both deeply fulfilling and overflowing with money. The reality is that many profitable niches may not be your dream come true, but they offer a solid foundation for building a successful business.

. **The Skillset Shuffle:** We often overlook the skills and knowledge we already possess. Just because a niche doesn't perfectly align with your hobbies doesn't mean you can't leverage your existing skills to build a thriving business within it.

"Niche Mastery" challenges the "perfect passion" myth. It helps you shift your focus from chasing fleeting excitement to identifying profitable niches that align with your skills, interests, and current market needs.

Think of it like this: Imagine a vast diamond mine. While some diamonds might be flawless and dazzling, others may be slightly cloudy or have unique inclusions. But a skilled jeweler knows that even these "imperfect" diamonds can be cut and polished into beautiful pieces with immense value.

Similarly, profitable niches don't have to be your ultimate passion. They can be areas where your existing skills and interests intersect with market demand. "Niche Mastery" is your guide to unearthing these hidden gems, the diamonds in the rough, that hold the key to building a successful and fulfilling online business.

Let's move beyond the myth of the "perfect passion" and unlock the true profit potential that lies within you.

Analysis Paralysis Prison: Why You're Stuck and How to Escape with Action

*I*magine a sculptor staring at a massive block of marble, paralyzed by the endless possibilities. Every chisel stroke could be a mistake, every chip a permanent scar. Fear of imperfection keeps the sculptor frozen, the masterpiece forever trapped within the stone.

This, my friend, is the analysis paralysis prison that plagues aspiring online entrepreneurs. We spend hours researching, and analyzing every niche, every strategy, every **"guru's"** advice. We become overwhelmed by the sheer volume of information, and the constant pressure to make the "perfect" choice. But in this relentless pursuit of perfection, we lose sight of the most crucial element: action.

Here's why analysis paralysis keeps you stuck in the online wilderness:

- **The Information Avalanche**: The internet drowns us in a constant flow of "how-to" guides, niche suggestions, and conflicting marketing strategies. This information overload fuels overthinking, making it impossible to choose a direction and take action.

- **The Fear of Failure**: Analysis paralysis often stems from a crippling fear of failure. We dissect every potential niche, searching for any hint that might lead to an unsuccessful outcome. This fear keeps us rooted in our comfort zone, preventing the very growth and learning that comes from taking action.

- **The Perfection Trap:** The quest for the "**perfect niche**", the "**perfect strategy**", and the "**perfect launch**" hinders progress. We become so focused on getting everything right that we never actually begin.

"Niche Mastery" isn't another analysis paralysis enabler. It's a call to action, a guide that empowers you to break free from the prison of overthinking and embrace the power of doing.

Think of it like this: A skilled artist doesn't wait for the "perfect" idea to strike before picking up a brush. They start with a rough sketch, and a loose plan, and then learn and refine as they go. The masterpiece isn't born from paralysis; it's born from the action of creating.

"Niche Mastery" provides you with that initial sketch, a framework for identifying a profitable niche that aligns with your interests and skills. But more importantly, it teaches you to embrace imperfect action. It shows you how to take that first step, learn from experience, and continuously refine your approach.

Stop waiting for the "perfect" moment. Let "Niche Mastery" be your chisel, the tool that helps you break free from the analysis paralysis prison and begin sculpting your online business success story, one imperfect yet impactful action at a time.

PART 1: THE NICHE MASTERY FRAMEWORK - A DEEP DIVE

CHAPTER 1

DEMYSTIFYING THE NICHE MASTERY: UNDERSTANDING BECKLER'S CORE CONCEPTS

Inexperience as an Asset: How a Beginner's Mindset Fuels Niche Discovery

Miles Beckler's Niche Mastery framework throws a curveball at conventional wisdom. It suggests that **"inexperience can actually be an advantage"** when it comes to identifying a profitable online niche. This might sound counterintuitive, but here's why it holds weight:

- **Fresh Eyes and Untapped Potential**: Seasoned entrepreneurs often get caught up in industry trends and established markets. Beginners, on the other hand, approach the online landscape with fresh eyes, free from preconceived notions. This allows them to identify hidden gems – niches with untapped potential that experienced players might overlook.
- **Curiosity and Openness:** Newcomers bring a natural sense of curiosity to the table. They're not afraid to ask questions, explore unconventional niches, and experiment with different approaches. This openness can lead to the discovery of lucrative niche markets that wouldn't have been considered by someone stuck in a "been there, done that" mindset.
- **Less Baggage, More Agility:** Experienced entrepreneurs often carry baggage from past failures or limiting beliefs. Beginners, on the other hand, are unburdened by these

experiences. They're more willing to take calculated risks, pivot strategies quickly, and adapt to changing market conditions. This agility is crucial for success in the ever-evolving online world.

But how do you leverage inexperience as an asset? Here are some tips:

. **Embrace the "Beginner's Mind":** Approach niche selection with childlike curiosity. Ask questions, explore different possibilities, and don't be afraid to venture outside your comfort zone.

. **Focus on Problems, Not Industries:** Instead of getting caught up in established industries, look for problems people are facing in their daily lives. Can you offer a unique solution within a specific niche, regardless of its current market presence?

. **Challenge Assumptions:** Don't be afraid to question industry norms. **Just because a niche seems "too small" or "not competitive** enough" doesn't mean it doesn't hold potential.

Remember, inexperience isn't a weakness; it's a blank canvas. The Niche Mastery framework equips you with the tools to paint a masterpiece on that canvas – a profitable online business built on a niche you discovered with the fresh perspective of a beginner.

The next sub-chapter will delve deeper into the core concepts of the Niche Mastery, including the "**Profit Potential Formula**" and how to assess the viability of a niche idea. So, embrace your beginner's mind, and let's get started on your niche discovery journey.

The Three Pillars of a Profitable Niche: Passion, Profit, and Audience

*M*iles Beckler's Niche Mastery framework rests upon three fundamental pillars

– a sturdy triangle that supports a thriving online business. These pillars are:

- **Passion:** The fuel that ignites your creativity and drives your dedication. Without a spark of passion for your niche, content creation becomes a chore, and marketing feels like pushing a boulder uphill.
- **Profit:** The lifeblood of your online business. Your chosen niche must have the potential to generate revenue, whether through affiliate marketing, selling your own products, or offering services.
- **Audience:** The heart of your business. A profitable niche thrives because it resonates with a specific audience that has a need for your expertise and solutions.

Imagine these three pillars as the legs of a stool. If any one leg is missing or weak, the entire structure collapses. Here's why each pillar is crucial:

Passion:

- **Authenticity and Engagement:** Passion fuels authentic content that resonates with your audience. Your enthusiasm shines through, fostering trust and connection with potential customers.
- **Motivation and Persistence:** Building an online business takes time and effort. Passion is the fire that keeps you going through the inevitable challenges and setbacks.
- **Innovation and Creativity:** A genuine interest in your niche fuels constant learning and innovation. It allows you to develop unique solutions and stand out in a crowded marketplace.

Profit:
- **Sustainability and Growth:** Profitability ensures the long-term viability of your online business. It allows you to reinvest in growth, develop new offerings, and ultimately achieve your financial goals.
- **Market Validation:** A niche with profit potential indicates a real need in the

marketplace. People are willing to pay for solutions that showcase the validity of your chosen area.
- **Focus and Direction:** The pursuit of profit helps you refine your niche and target specific audience pain points, ensuring your content and offerings deliver true value.

Audience:
- **Relevance and Impact:** Focusing on a specific audience allows you to tailor your content and offerings to their exact needs and challenges. This ensures your message resonates and creates a real impact.
- **Community Building:** A well-defined audience fosters a sense of community around your niche. This loyal following fuels engagement amplifies your reach, and creates brand advocates.
- **Market Research and Targeting:** Understanding your audience allows you to conduct targeted market research,

identify their buying habits, and develop marketing strategies that convert them into paying customers.

The Niche Mastery isn't about prioritizing one pillar over the others. It's about finding the sweet spot where your passion intersects with a profitable niche that has a dedicated audience.

CHAPTER 2:

THE PROFIT POTENTIAL FORMULA: DECODING NICHE PROFITABILITY

Breaking Down the Formula: Demand, Competition, and Affiliate Programs

You've identified a niche that sparks your passion and caters to a specific audience. But before you dive headfirst into content creation, there's one crucial question: Is this niche profitable? The Niche Mastery equips you with a powerful tool to answer this question – the Profit Potential Formula.

Here's how it works:
Profit Potential = (DEMAND x COMPETITION) x AFFILIATE PROGRAMS

Let us dissect every component of the formula.:

1. DEMAND: This measures the interest level for your chosen niche. Is there a real need for your expertise and solutions within the target audience? Here are some ways to assess demand:

- **Keyword Research:** Analyze search volume for relevant keywords. High search volume indicates a healthy level of interest in your niche.
- **Social Listening:** Monitor online communities and social media groups to see what problems your target audience is discussing. Are there recurring themes and pain points you can address?
- **Market Research Reports:** Industry reports and trend analyses can provide valuable insights into the size and growth potential of your target market.

2. COMPETITION: This assesses the level of competition within your niche. How many established players are there? While some competition is healthy, a saturated market with dominant players can make it difficult to stand out. Here's how to gauge competition:

- **Market Saturation:** Analyze the number of existing websites, blogs, and online courses related to your niche.
- **Content Quality:** Evaluate the quality of content produced by your competitors. Are there gaps in their approach that you can exploit?
- **Marketing Strategies:** Research how your competitors are reaching their audience. Is there an opportunity to employ different marketing tactics and carve out a unique space within the niche?

3. AFFILIATE PROGRAMS: Not all niches are created equal. Some offer a wider variety of **high-paying affiliate programs** than others. Affiliate programs allow you to earn commissions by promoting relevant products and services to your audience.

Here are some tips for evaluating affiliate programs within your niche:

- **Commission Rates:** Seek out programs that offer competitive commission structures in terms of rates. Higher commission rates translate to greater potential profits.
- **Cookie Duration:** Longer cookie durations mean you have more time to earn a commission after someone clicks on your affiliate link.
- **Program Reputation:** Choose reputable programs with a track record of good customer service and timely payouts.

By analyzing each element of the Profit Potential Formula, you get a clearer picture of the **financial viability** of your chosen niche. **Remember, the ideal niche lands in the sweet spot where there's enough demand to support**

a healthy audience, manageable competition to allow for growth, and access to lucrative affiliate programs to generate revenue.

The next sub-chapter will provide you with worksheets and templates to help you apply the Profit Potential Formula to your niche ideas. Don't just pick a niche based on passion alone; use this formula to ensure your enthusiasm is fueled by the potential for real profitability.

Worksheets & Templates: Putting the Formula into Action

Now that you understand the three key elements of the Profit Potential Formula – Demand, Competition, and Affiliate Programs – it's time to roll up your sleeves and put it into action! This chapter provides you with essential worksheets and templates to guide you through assessing the profitability of your niche ideas.

WORKSHEET 1: NICHE BRAINSTORMING

- **List 10 Potential Niches:** Brainstorm a variety of niche ideas that spark your interest and align with your skills and experience.
- **Target Audience for Each Niche:** For each niche, identify the specific audience you would be catering to. Who are you trying to help?
- **Passion Meter (1-10):** Rate your level of passion for each niche idea on a scale of 1 (low) to 10 (high).

WORKSHEET 2: DEMAND ANALYSIS

- **Niche (from Worksheet 1):** Choose one niche idea you'd like to analyze further.
- **Relevant Keywords:** List 5-10 keywords that represent your chosen niche.
- **Search Volume (for each keyword):** Use free keyword research tools to estimate the monthly search volume for each keyword.

- **Social Listening Platforms (List 2):** Identify two relevant online communities or social media groups where your target audience congregates.
- **Recurring Audience Issues (from Social Listening):** Based on your observations, list 3 common challenges or pain points faced by your target audience.

WORKSHEET 3: COMPETITION ANALYSIS

- **Niche (from Worksheet 2):** Refer back to the niche you chose for demand analysis.
- **Competing Websites (List 3):** Identify three main competitors within your niche.
- **Content Quality Assessment (Briefly describe the quality and focus of each competitor's content):** Analyze the quality of content produced by your competitors. Are there any gaps or areas where you can offer a unique perspective?
- **Marketing Strategies (List 2):** Identify two main marketing channels used by

your competitors (e.g., social media marketing, email marketing).

WORKSHEET 4: AFFILIATE PROGRAM RESEARCH

- **Niche (from Worksheet 3):** Refer back to the niche you've been analyzing.
- **Potential Affiliate Programs (List 3):** Research and list three potential affiliate programs relevant to your niche.
- **Commission Rate (for each program):** Find out the commission rate offered by each program (expressed as a percentage of the sale price).
- **Cookie Duration (for each program):** Determine the cookie duration for each program (e.g., 30 days, 90 days).

Template: Profit Potential Scorecard

- Niche:
- Demand Score (Average of Search Volume + Social Listening Observations):

- Competition Score (1-10, with 10 being the most competitive):
- Affiliate Program Score (Average of Commission Rate + Cookie Duration):
- Overall Profit Potential Score (Average of Demand Score, Competition Score, and Affiliate Program Score):

Using the Worksheets and Template:

1. Complete the worksheets for each niche idea you're considering.
2. Use the Profit Potential Scorecard to assign a score based on your findings for each element of the formula.
3. The higher your Overall Profit Potential Score, the greater the potential for profitability within that niche.

Remember: The Profit Potential Formula is a valuable tool, but it's not the only factor to consider. Don't discard a niche solely because of a lower score. There might be other revenue streams beyond affiliate programs, or

your unique approach could allow you to carve out a space within a competitive market.

THE KEY TAKEAWAY:

By using these worksheets and the Profit Potential Formula, you're making data-driven decisions about your niche selection. You're moving beyond guesswork and passion alone, and incorporating a layer of financial viability analysis into your online business journey.

CHAPTER 3:

BEYOND THE BOOK: UNVEILING HIDDEN NICHES

Exploring Untapped Markets: Strategies for Identifying Niche Opportunities

The Niche Mastery framework equips you with powerful tools, but the online world is an ever-evolving landscape. What if the "perfect" niche you identified today becomes saturated tomorrow? Don't worry! This chapter goes beyond the book, providing you with strategies to become a niche explorer, constantly uncovering hidden gems with high-profit potential.

Exploring Untapped Markets:.

Forget the "get rich quick" niche lists flooding the internet. Here's how to find hidden niches with genuine audience needs and room for growth:

. **Follow Your Curiosity:** Passion is crucial, but so is genuine curiosity. Look beyond established industries and explore topics that pique your interest. Could you offer a unique perspective on a seemingly mundane hobby or solve a problem within a subculture?

. **Think Micro-niches:** Don't be afraid to zoom in. Large niches often present overwhelming competition. By focusing on a micro-niche – a hyper-specific segment within a broader niche – you cater to a highly engaged audience with less competition.

. **Problem-Solution Lens:** Shift your perspective. Look for problems people face in their daily lives, both online and offline. Can you offer a solution through your knowledge, skills, or experiences, regardless of the niche's current market presence?

Strategies for Uncovering Hidden Niches:

. **Social Listening on Niche Platforms:** Dive deeper than mainstream social media. Explore dedicated forums, online communities, and niche social media platforms where your target audience congregates. Listen to their conversations, identify recurring problems, and brainstorm solutions.

. **Trending Topics with Long-Term Potential:** Jump on trends, but with a twist. Analyze trending topics with long-term potential, then identify specific sub-niches within the trend that haven't been fully saturated.

. **Industry Shifts and Emerging Technologies:** Stay informed about industry shifts and emerging technologies. These disruptions often create new needs and pain points, offering opportunities for niche entrepreneurs to offer solutions before the market becomes overcrowded.

Remember:

- **Focus on Value, Not Just Passion:** While passion is important, prioritize niches

where your skills and expertise can deliver real value to a specific audience.
- **Be a Trendsetter, Not a Follower:** Don't chase established niches. Become a trendsetter by identifying hidden opportunities and educating your audience about the value you can offer.
- **Embrace Continuous Learning:** The online world is constantly evolving. Stay curious, keep learning, and refine your niche exploration skills over time.

This chapter is your passport to a world beyond the readily available niche lists. By adopting the mindset of a niche explorer and utilizing these strategies, you'll be well on your way to uncovering hidden gems – profitable niches that are perfectly suited for your unique blend of passion, skills, and the evolving market landscape. The journey to online business success is a continuous exploration, and the Niche Mastery empowers you to be a constant discoverer, forever unearthing new opportunities for growth and fulfillment.

Case Studies & Reader Success Stories: Real-World Examples of Niche Mastery Triumphs

The Niche Mastery isn't just a theoretical framework; it's a roadmap to success for everyday people like you. This chapter showcases real-world examples of individuals who leveraged the power of niche exploration to build thriving online businesses.

Case Study 1: From Corporate Escapee to Micro-Influencer - The Sustainable Candle niche

Sarah, a former corporate drone yearning for creative freedom, discovered her niche through Niche Mastery's focus on problem-solving. While researching eco-friendly living, she stumbled upon a gap in the market – a lack of resources for busy individuals seeking non-toxic, sustainable candle options.

Her Niche: Sustainable and Ethical Candle Making for Health-Conscious Millennials.

Niche Mastery in Action:

- **Passion & Problem-Solution:** Sarah's interest in healthy living intersected with a problem faced by her target audience – the prevalence of paraffin-based candles with harmful toxins.
- **Micro-niche Exploration:** Instead of focusing on the broad "candle-making" niche, she zoomed in on the eco-conscious aspect, attracting a specific audience with aligned values.
- **Profit Potential:** By partnering with reputable sustainable candle companies and leveraging affiliate marketing, Sarah built a profitable online business while promoting a cause she cared about.

Case Study 2: The Accidental Entrepreneur - The Forgotten History of Baking

David, a history buff with a passion for baking, never intended to become an online entrepreneur. However, after attending a Niche

Mastery workshop, he realized the potential of his unique knowledge.

His Niche: Historical Baking Techniques and Recipes for Modern Enthusiasts.

Niche Mastery in Action:
- **Curiosity & Untapped Market:** David's fascination with forgotten historical recipes sparked a niche idea with untapped potential.
- **Value Proposition:** He offered a unique blend of historical knowledge and practical baking techniques, catering to a niche audience seeking to recreate authentic historical recipes.
- **Beyond Affiliate Programs:** David monetized his niche by creating online courses, ebooks, and historical baking kits, demonstrating the diverse revenue streams possible within a well-defined niche.

Reader Success Stories:

These are just a few examples. Niche Mastery's online community is brimming with success stories from individuals who discovered hidden niches and built thriving online businesses:

- A former accountant leveraged her love for urban gardening to create a profitable blog on balcony vegetable gardens for city dwellers.
- A stay-at-home mom with a background in art history parlayed her knowledge into a niche website offering online courses on identifying and appraising antique furniture.
- A fitness enthusiast with a knack for storytelling built a loyal following by creating workout routines inspired by historical figures like Spartan warriors and medieval knights.

THE KEY TAKEAWAY:
The possibilities are endless. By embracing the principles of niche exploration outlined in this chapter and throughout the Niche

Mastery, you too can become a success story. Remember, the most profitable niches often lie hidden in plain sight, waiting to be discovered by curious minds armed with the right tools and strategies.

NICHE MASTERY IN ACTION

PART 2: VALIDATING YOUR NICHE - FROM SPARK TO CERTAINTY

CHAPTER 4:

ACTIONABLE VALIDATION TECHNIQUES: MOVING BEYOND THE ONE-HOUR MARK

Competitor Analysis: Understanding the Landscape and Identifying Gaps

Congratulations! You've identified a niche that sparks your passion and holds potential for profitability. But before you dive headfirst into content creation, there's one crucial step: competitor analysis. This chapter equips you with actionable validation techniques to move beyond the one-hour mark and conduct a thorough analysis of your competitive landscape.

Why Does Competitor Analysis Matters?

Understanding your competition is like having a roadmap of the battlefield. It allows you to:

. **Identify Gaps and Opportunities:** By analyzing your competitors' strengths and weaknesses, you can identify gaps in their offerings and carve out a unique space within the niche.

. **Learn from Their Successes (and Failures):** Competitor analysis allows you to learn from their best practices and avoid replicating their mistakes.

. **Develop a Winning Strategy:** Understanding your competition empowers you to craft a targeted marketing strategy that positions you for success.

Moving Beyond Basic Website Analysis:

Sure, you can visit your competitors' websites and get a general sense of their content and offerings. But for a deeper understanding, you need to go beyond the surface level. Here are some actionable validation techniques:

. **Content Audit:** Analyze your competitors' content in detail. What topics do they cover? What formats do they use (articles, videos, podcasts)? Are there any recurring themes or gaps in their content strategy?

. **Customer Reviews and Feedback:** Read customer reviews and online conversations about your competitors' products and services. What are people praising? What are their common frustrations? These insights can help you tailor your offerings to address specific customer pain points.

. **Engagement Metrics:** Look beyond follower count. Analyze engagement metrics like comments, shares, and click-through rates on your competitors' social media posts and blog content. This can reveal what resonates with the audience and what kind of content generates the most interest.

. Free Products and Trials: If your competitors offer free trials, webinars, or downloadable resources, take advantage of them! Experience their offerings firsthand and identify areas where you can provide a better user experience or more value.

Identifying Gaps and Opportunities:

Once you've conducted a thorough competitor analysis, it's time to translate your findings into actionable insights. Here's how:

. Content Gaps: Look for areas where your competitors' content is lacking in depth, outdated, or simply not engaging. This presents an opportunity for you to create high-quality content that fills those gaps and attracts your target audience.

. Target Audience Misunderstandings: Sometimes, competitors unintentionally confuse their audience with overly complex explanations or jargon. You can position yourself as the "clarity expert" by presenting information in a clear, concise, and easy-to-understand manner.

. **Underexploited Formats:** Perhaps your competitors primarily focus on written content. You can differentiate yourself by incorporating engaging video tutorials, infographics, or interactive quizzes to cater to different learning styles within your audience.

Remember: Competitor analysis isn't about copying what others are doing. It's about learning from them, identifying opportunities, and developing a strategy that allows you to stand out in a crowded marketplace.

Beyond the Google Search: Unmasking Your Ideal Audience

*Y*ou've identified a niche that ignites your passion and shows promise for profitability. You've analyzed your competitors, uncovering their strengths, weaknesses, and potential gaps in their approach. But there's one crucial missing piece – a deep understanding of your **ideal audience,** equipping you with actionable validation techniques to truly **Unmask Your Ideal Audience.** By gaining a deeper understanding of their needs, desires, and pain points, you can tailor your niche approach to perfectly resonate with them, fostering a loyal following and building a thriving online business.

Why Audience Research Matters?

Imagine crafting beautiful content and launching an impeccable marketing campaign, only to discover it falls flat with your target audience. **Audience research prevents this scenario**. It allows you to:

. **Speak Their Language:** By understanding your audience's terminology, pain points, and preferred communication styles, you can craft content that resonates on a deeper level.

. **Solve Their Problems:** Effective audience research helps you identify the specific challenges your ideal customer faces within your chosen niche. Your content and offerings can then be positioned as the ultimate solutions.

. **Build Trust and Rapport:** When you demonstrate a genuine understanding of your audience's struggles and aspirations, you build trust and establish yourself as a credible authority within the niche.

Moving Beyond the Google Search:

Sure, basic demographics and keyword research can provide a starting point. But to truly understand your ideal audience, you need to dig deeper and move beyond the one-hour mark of a simple Google search. Here are some actionable validation techniques:

. **Targeted Online Communities:** Immerse yourself in online communities, forums, and social media groups frequented by your target audience. Participate in discussions, observe their interactions, and identify recurring themes and challenges they face.

. **Surveys and Questionnaires:** Craft targeted surveys and questionnaires to gather direct feedback from your ideal audience. Inquire about the individuals' areas of concern, deficiencies in knowledge, and preferable modes of learning.

. **One-on-One Interviews:** Take audience research a step further by conducting one-on-one interviews. This allows you to delve deeper into individual experiences, motivations, and buying behaviors within your niche.

. **Customer Reviews and Case Studies:** Analyze customer reviews of existing products and services within your niche. Look for common frustrations and identify areas where you can offer a superior solution or a more positive customer experience.

Unmasking Your Ideal Audience:

Once you've implemented these validation techniques, you'll be brimming with valuable insights. Here's how to translate them into actionable knowledge:

- **Develop a Customer Avatar:** Create a detailed profile of your ideal customer. This avatar should encompass their demographics, interests, challenges, and preferred ways of consuming information.

- **Content Tailoring:** Use your customer avatar to tailor your content strategy. Develop content formats, address specific pain points, and utilize language that resonates directly with your ideal audience.

- **Value Proposition Refinement:** Refine your value proposition based on your audience research. Clearly articulate how your niche expertise and offerings directly address their problems and fulfill their desires.

Remember: Audience research is an ongoing process. As your business grows and your

audience evolves, revisit these techniques to ensure your offerings remain relevant and continue to resonate with the people you're passionate about helping.

The next sub-chapter will explore the power of storytelling and community building, essential elements for attracting and retaining your ideal audience within your chosen niche. By combining actionable audience research with these powerful tools, you'll be well on your way to establishing a loyal following and building a thriving online business with a strong foundation for long-term success.

From Data to Narrative: The Power of Storytelling and Community Building

*Y*ou've identified a niche that sparks your passion and boasts profitability potential. You've analyzed your competitors, uncovering their strengths and weaknesses. You've delved deep into audience research, unmasking the desires and challenges of your ideal customer. Now it's time to bridge the gap between data and connection. This chapter equips you with powerful tools to move beyond the one-hour mark and leverage the art of storytelling and community building to attract, engage, and retain your ideal audience within your chosen niche.

Why Storytelling and Community Matter?

In today's information overload, data points and statistics alone can't win hearts and minds. Storytelling breathes life into your niche expertise. It allows you to:

. **Connect on an Emotional Level:** Facts tell, but stories sell. By weaving narratives that resonate with your audience's aspirations and struggles, you foster emotional connections that go beyond dry data.

. **Make Information Memorable:** People remember stories, not statistics. By presenting complex information within a compelling narrative framework, you increase knowledge retention and engagement with your content.

. Establish Authority and Credibility: Sharing your own experiences and challenges within your niche story positions you as a relatable guide, not just a distant expert.

Community Building: The Foundation for Long-Term Success

Building a community around your niche goes beyond follower counts. It's about fostering a space for connection, shared experiences, and mutual support. A flourishing virtual community enables one to:

. Boost Engagement and Interaction: When your audience feels like part of a community, they're more likely to participate in discussions, ask questions, and share their own experiences, keeping your content and brand top-of-mind.

. Generate User-Generated Content: A strong community encourages your audience to become brand advocates. Testimonials, reviews, and social media shares from satisfied customers become powerful marketing tools, expanding your reach organically.

. **Gain Valuable Feedback:** Your online community provides a direct line of communication with your audience. By actively listening to their feedback and suggestions, you can continuously refine your approach and ensure your offerings remain aligned with their evolving needs.

Actionable Techniques for Storytelling and Community Building:

. **Craft Compelling Narratives:** Infuse your content with personal stories, case studies, and anecdotes that illustrate the challenges and triumphs within your niche.

. **Embrace Multiple Content Formats:** Utilize storytelling through various formats like blog posts, videos, podcasts, and even infographics. Adapt to various learning approaches and maintain the interest of your audience.

. **Facilitate Two-Way Communication:** Respond to comments, answer questions, and actively participate in discussions within your online community.

. **Host Interactive Events:** Organize live Q&A sessions, webinars, or online challenges to foster engagement and a sense of community spirit.

. **Encourage User-Generated Content:** Run contests, ask for feedback, and incentivize your audience to share their experiences related to your niche.

Remember: Storytelling and community building are ongoing processes. As you create content, engage with your audience, and refine your approach, the narrative of your brand and the strength of your community will continue to evolve.

Understanding Keyword Research:

Keyword research is the foundation of any successful online content strategy. It's the process of identifying the words and phrases people use to search for information online. By understanding these keywords, you can:

. **Target the Right Audience:** Craft content that directly addresses your ideal audience's needs and interests.

. **Improve Search Engine Ranking (SEO):** Optimize your website and content to rank higher in search engine results for relevant keywords.

. **Drive Organic Traffic:** Attract more visitors to your website or online platform through organic search.

Types of Keyword Research Tools:

There are numerous paid and complimentary keyword research instruments available. Here are some popular options:

1. **Free Keyword Research Tools:**
   - **Google Trends:** Analyzes search trends over time and across different locations.

- **Answer the Public:** Suggest questions people are asking related to your seed keyword.
- **Keywordtool.io:** Provides suggestions for long-tail keywords and search volume estimates.

2. **Paid Keyword Research Tools:**
   - **Ahrefs:** Offers comprehensive keyword research data with search volume, competition level, and keyword difficulty.
   - **SEMrush:** Provides in-depth keyword research features along with competitor analysis and backlink tracking.
   - **Moz Pro:** Offers keyword research tools with a focus on SEO difficulty and content gap analysis.

Using Keyword Research Tools Effectively:

Here are some tips for using keyword research tools to your advantage:

. **Start with Seed Keywords:** Identify broad keywords representing your niche.

. **Expand with Long-Tail Keywords:** Refine your research by focusing on longer, more specific keyword phrases with lower competition.

. **Analyze Search Volume:** Consider the balance between search volume (how often a keyword is searched for) and competition level.

. **Explore Related Searches:** Identify additional keyword ideas suggested by the tool.

. **Target User Intent:** Go beyond just the keyword itself, and understand the intent behind the search (informational, transactional, etc.).

Benefits of Keyword Research Tools:

Here's how keyword research tools can benefit your online presence:

. **Save Time:** Tools automate the keyword research process, saving you valuable time and effort.

. **Data-Driven Decisions:** Make informed content creation decisions based on real search data.

- **Uncover Hidden Gems:** Discover long-tail keywords with high potential and lower competition.
- **Stay Ahead of Trends:** Identify emerging topics and adapt your content strategy accordingly.

Remember: Keyword research is an ongoing process. Regularly revisit your keyword research to ensure your content remains relevant and aligns with evolving search trends and audience interests.

Beyond Keyword Research Tools:

While keyword research tools are valuable, don't solely rely on them. Consider these additional elements:

- **Analysis of Competitors:** Determine which keywords your rivals are utilizing.
- **Social Listening:** Monitor online conversations within your niche to understand audience interest.

. **Industry Reports**: Stay updated on industry trends and emerging keywords.

By combining keyword research tools with these additional strategies, you'll gain a well-rounded understanding of your target audience and the keywords that resonate most effectively within your chosen niche.

Engaging with Online Communities: Validating Niche Ideas Through Interaction

*Y*ou've identified a niche that sparks your passion and profitability potential. You've analyzed your competitors, uncovering their strengths and weaknesses. You've delved into audience research, unmasking the desires and challenges of your ideal customer. Now it's time to take your validation efforts a step further by leveraging the power of online communities.

Moving Beyond the Google Search: The Power of Online Interaction

While keyword research and surveys offer valuable data, there's no substitute for real-time interaction with your target audience. **Engaging with online communities** allows you to move beyond the one-hour mark of basic research and dive deep into the conversations, challenges, and interests that truly define your niche. Here's how online communities can be powerful validation tools:

. **Authentic Audience Insights:** Online communities are spaces where people freely discuss their problems, share experiences, and celebrate successes. By actively participating, you gain unfiltered insights directly from your ideal audience.

. **Validating Niche Demand:** Does your niche idea resonate with a real community online? The level of activity, discussion threads, and overall engagement within relevant online communities can be strong indicators of potential audience interest.

- **Identifying Content Gaps:** Pay close attention to recurring questions, unresolved issues, and topics that generate passionate debate within online communities. These gaps represent opportunities for you to create high-value content that directly addresses your audience's needs.

Key Platforms for Engaging with Online Communities:

The online world offers a vast landscape of niche-specific communities. The following are some well-known platforms that can serve as starting points:

- **Forums:** Many niches have dedicated online forums where enthusiasts gather to discuss topics, share resources, and troubleshoot problems.
- **Social Media Groups:** Look for Facebook groups, LinkedIn groups, or niche-specific

communities on other social media platforms where your target audience congregates.

.   **Discord Servers:** Discord has become a popular platform for online communities, particularly within gaming, tech, and creative niches.

.   **Subreddits:** The vast world of Reddit offers subreddits dedicated to almost every imaginable niche. Find yours and immerse yourself in the conversations.

Strategies for Effective Engagement:

Here's how to ensure your participation in online communities is not only informative but also validates your niche idea:

.   **Become a Valued Contributor:** Don't just lurk in the shadows; actively participate in discussions. Share your knowledge, answer questions thoughtfully, and offer helpful advice.

.   **Listen More Than You Speak:** Pay close attention to the conversations, challenges, and frustrations expressed within the community.

This will provide invaluable insights for shaping your niche approach.

- **Ask Open-Ended Questions**: Don't be afraid to ask questions to spark discussion and gauge audience interest in specific aspects of your niche idea.
- **Avoid Self-Promotion:** While you can subtly mention your niche interests, focus on building genuine connections and providing value to the community.

Transforming Online Interaction into Actionable Insights:

Once you've actively engaged with online communities, it's time to translate your observations into actionable insights:

- **Refine Your Niche Focus:** The conversations within online communities might reveal a sub-niche with even greater potential or a specific aspect of your niche that deserves more focus.
- **Content Brainstorming:** Use the discussions, questions, and challenges you encounter as

springboards for creating high-value content that directly addresses your audience's needs.

. **Develop Your Value Proposition:** By understanding the specific pain points and aspirations voiced within the community, you can refine your value proposition to resonate more powerfully with your ideal audience.

Remember: Engaging with online communities is an ongoing process. As your niche evolves and your understanding deepens, continue to participate in these valuable spaces. This will ensure your approach remains relevant, your content addresses current needs, and your business continues to thrive within a community you've helped to cultivate.

CHAPTER 5:

OVERCOMING NICHE SELECTION ROADBLOCKS: MINDSET SHIFTS AND SOLUTIONS

Taming the Fear of Failure: Embracing Experimentation in Niche Selection

*Y*ou've embarked on the exciting journey of carving your niche in the online world. However, the path to success is rarely linear. This chapter equips you with the tools to overcome a common roadblock – the fear of failure – and instead, embrace experimentation as a powerful strategy for niche selection.

The Fear of Failure: A Paralyzing Force

The fear of failure can be a formidable foe, preventing you from taking the first step towards your niche selection. Here's why it's crucial to overcome this fear:

. **Analysis Paralysis:** Overthinking and fearing failure can lead to analysis paralysis, keeping you stuck in the research phase and hindering progress.
. **Missed Opportunities:** The online world is dynamic. By clinging to the fear of failure, you might miss out on emerging niches with high-growth potential.
. **Limited Learning:** Experimentation is a key driver of learning. Fearing failure prevents you from testing your ideas, gathering valuable data, and refining your niche approach.

Embracing Experimentation: A Growth Mindset

Shift your perspective from fearing failure to embracing experimentation. Here's why this approach is empowering:

. **Validation Through Testing:** The best way to validate your niche idea is to put it out into the world and see how your target audience responds.

- **Learning from Every Step:** Every experiment, successful or not, offers valuable lessons. Use them to refine your niche focus and content strategy.
- **Building Resilience:** Experimentation fosters resilience. By overcoming initial hurdles and adapting your approach, you build the mental toughness required for long-term online business success.

Strategies for Experimentation in Niche Selection:

Here are some practical ways to embrace experimentation and overcome the fear of failure in niche selection:

- **Start Small, Scale Later:** Don't feel pressured to launch a full-fledged website or online course right away. Begin with a micro-niche blog, a social media experiment, or a short ebook to test the waters.

. **Content as a Testing Ground:** Create niche-specific content like blog posts, infographics, or videos and gauge audience response through engagement metrics and feedback.

. **Minimum Viable Product (MVP):** Develop a Minimum Viable Product (MVP) – a basic version of your offering – to test its viability within your target audience before investing significant resources.

. **Freelancing and Consulting:** Offer freelance services or consulting within your niche to gain practical experience, refine your value proposition, and validate audience interest.

Remember: Experimentation is an ongoing process. As you gather data, receive feedback, and learn from your experiences, be prepared to adapt your niche focus and iterate on your approach. Here are some additional tips for navigating experimentation:

- **Set SMART Goals:** Establish Specific, Measurable, Achievable, Relevant, and

Time-Bound goals for your niche experiments to track progress and measure success.
- **Embrace Feedback:** Don't shy away from constructive criticism. Use feedback from your audience to identify areas for improvement and refine your niche strategy.
- **Celebrate Small Wins:** Acknowledge and celebrate even minor victories during your experimentation phase. These wins will keep you motivated and fuel your drive to continue iterating.

Imposter Syndrome and the "Shiny Object Syndrome": Strategies to Stay Focused

The path to niche selection is rarely smooth sailing. This chapter tackles two common roadblocks: Imposter Syndrome and the "Shiny Object Syndrome." We'll explore how to overcome these challenges and maintain focus on building a thriving niche business.

Imposter Syndrome: Doubting Your Expertise

Imposter Syndrome can cripple even the most capable individuals. It manifests as a persistent feeling of inadequacy, despite your skills and knowledge. Here's why it's important to address Imposter Syndrome:

- **Paralyzed Progress:** Doubting your abilities can prevent you from taking action and launching your niche business.

- **Diminished Confidence:** Imposter Syndrome can erode your confidence, making it difficult to market yourself and connect with your ideal audience.

- **Focus on Competition:** It can lead to an unhealthy focus on what others are doing, hindering your ability to develop your unique voice and approach within your niche.

Combating Imposter Syndrome:

. **Focus on Value, Not Perfection:** Shift your focus from achieving perfection to offering value to your target audience. Your passion and genuine desire to help can be even more powerful than having all the answers.

. **Commemorate Your Accomplishments:** Recognize your achievements, regardless of their magnitude. Building a business takes time and effort. Recognize your accomplishments and celebrate each milestone.

. **Connect with Like-Minded Individuals:** Surround yourself with supportive individuals who believe in you and your niche vision.

"Shiny Object Syndrome": Chasing the Next Big Thing

The online world is full of "shiny objects" – new niche ideas, marketing tactics, and business opportunities. The "Shiny Object Syndrome" is the constant urge to chase the latest trend, leading to scattered efforts and hindering progress within your chosen niche.

Why It Matters:
- Scattered Focus: Jumping from one niche idea to the next prevents you from developing deep expertise and building a targeted audience.
- Wasted Resources: Investing time and energy in fleeting trends can divert resources away from building a sustainable business within your chosen niche.
- Feeling Overwhelmed: The constant pursuit of the "next big thing" can lead to information overload and feelings of overwhelm.

Staying Focused on Your Niche:
. **Align Passion with Profit:** Choose a niche that aligns with your interests and passions. This intrinsic motivation will help you stay focused during inevitable challenges.

. **Set Clear Goals:** Establish clear, achievable goals for your niche business. Having a roadmap will keep you on track and prevent distractions from derailing your progress.

● **Embrace Continuous Learning:** While staying focused on your niche, dedicate time to learning and refining your skills within that specific area.

Remember: Building a successful niche business takes time, dedication, and perseverance. By overcoming Imposter Syndrome, avoiding the allure of the "Shiny Object Syndrome," and embracing the power of experimentation, you'll be well-equipped to navigate the challenges, maintain focus, and propel your niche business toward long-term success.

What if My Niche is Too Small? The Power of Micro-Niches in a Saturated Market

The fear of a niche being "too small" is a common concern. However, this chapter will challenge that perception and demonstrate the power of micro-niching within a saturated market.

The Micro-Niche Advantage:

While broad niches might seem more appealing initially, there are significant advantages to focusing on a micro-niche:

. **Reduced Competition:** Micro-niches face less competition, allowing you to stand out more easily and establish yourself as a niche authority.

. **Deeper Audience Connection:** By catering to a highly specific audience, you can develop a deeper understanding of their needs, challenges, and preferred communication styles.

. **Increased Engagement:** Micro-niche communities are often tight-knit and highly engaged. This fosters loyalty and repeat business for your niche offerings.

. **Premium Pricing Potential:** By becoming a recognized expert within your micro-niche, you have the potential to command premium pricing for your expertise and solutions.

Identifying Profitable Micro-Niches: Not all micro-niches are created equal. Here's how to identify a profitable micro-niche within a saturated market:

. **Passion Intersection:** Look for the intersection of your passions and interests with specific needs within a broader niche.

. **Problem-Solving Focus:** Identify a specific problem faced by a particular audience segment within the niche.

. **Growth Potential:** While the niche itself might be small, consider its growth trajectory. Is it a burgeoning trend with potential for audience expansion?

Examples of Powerful Micro-Niches:

Here are some examples to illustrate the potential of micro-niching:

- **Fitness Niche:** Broader Niche - Fitness. Micro-Niche - Fitness for busy moms over 40.
- Travel Niche: Broader Niche - Travel blogging. Micro-Niche - Luxury sustainable travel experiences in Southeast Asia.
- Pet Care Niche: Broader Niche - Dog training. Micro-Niche - Training service dogs for veterans with PTSD.

Remember: Don't be afraid to niche down further. A smaller, highly targeted audience can be incredibly powerful for building a loyal following and establishing a thriving online business

PART 3: BUILDING YOUR ONLINE BUSINESS - BONUS CHAPTER

CHAPTER 6:

FROM NICHE TO EMPIRE: THE INITIAL STEPS OF BUILDING YOUR ONLINE BUSINESS

Choosing a Business Model: Affiliate Marketing, E-commerce, or Beyond?

With your niche firmly established, it's time to translate your passion and expertise into a thriving online business. This chapter dives into the crucial first step: selecting the business model that best aligns with your niche, interests, and long-term goals.

The Business Model Landscape:

The online world offers a diverse range of business models. The following are three well-liked choices to assist you in commencing:

. **Affiliate Marketing:** Promote other people's products and earn a commission on each sale you generate. This is a low-risk approach ideal for beginners but relies heavily on effective marketing and audience trust.

. **E-commerce:** Sell physical or digital products directly to your audience. This model requires investment in inventory (physical products) or product creation (digital products) but offers higher profit margins and greater control over branding.

. **Coaching and Consulting:** Leverage your expertise to offer personalized services like coaching programs, consultations, or online courses. This model requires strong industry knowledge and effective communication skills but allows you to build high-value, recurring client relationships.

Choosing the Right Model for You:

Consider these factors when selecting your business model:

- **Niche Suitability:** Does the model align well with the products, services, or information you have to offer within your niche?
- **Resource Availability:** Do you have the financial resources for product creation (e-commerce) or initial marketing investments (affiliate marketing)?
- **Time Commitment:** How much time are you willing to dedicate to creating content, managing inventory, or delivering coaching services?
- **Skills and Interests:** Do you enjoy product creation (e-commerce), building marketing campaigns (affiliate marketing), or working directly with clients (coaching/consulting)?

Beyond the Big Three:

While affiliate marketing, e-commerce, and coaching/consulting are popular choices, there are other models to explore:

- **Membership sites:** provide paid members with special information, resources, or community access.
- **Freelancing:** Sell your skills and expertise directly to clients on a project-by-project basis.
- **Subscription Services:** Deliver ongoing value to subscribers through recurring payments for content or services.

Remember: Don't feel limited to just one model. You can combine elements of different approaches to create a hybrid business model that best suits your niche and goals.

Crafting Your Brand Identity: Standing Out in a Crowded Marketplace

Congratulations! You've identified your niche, overcome selection roadblocks, and chosen a business model to propel your online venture. Now it's time to craft your brand identity, the unique persona that will set you apart in a crowded marketplace and resonate deeply with your target audience.

Why does Brand Identity matter?

Your brand identity is more than just a logo and a color scheme. It's the essence of your business, encompassing your values, mission, and the experience you offer your audience. A strong brand identity:

.   **Attracts Your Ideal Audience:** A clear and compelling brand identity attracts customers who resonate with your values and offerings.

.   **Builds Trust and Credibility:** A consistent brand identity fosters trust and positions you as a reliable authority within your niche.

.   **Drives Customer Loyalty:** A strong brand identity fosters emotional connections and encourages customers to become loyal brand advocates.

Crafting Your Brand Story:

Your brand identity is built upon a compelling narrative. Here's how to craft your brand story:

. **Define Your Brand Values:** What core values define your business and guide your decision-making?
. **Identify Your Mission:** What problem are you solving or what need are you fulfilling within your niche?
. **Articulate Your Vision:** What do you aspire to achieve with your brand in the long term?

Building Your Brand Persona:

Imagine your brand as a person. Here's how to define its personality:
. **Voice and Tone:** How will you communicate with your audience? Formal, friendly, humorous, or something else entirely?
. **Visual Identity:** Develop a consistent visual language through your logo, color scheme, and website design that reflects your brand personality.

- **Brand Messaging:** Craft clear and concise messaging that conveys your value proposition and resonates with your target audience.

Making Your Brand Identity Tangible:

Now it's time to translate your brand story and persona into tangible elements:

- **Develop Your Brand Voice:** Ensure consistency in your writing style across all communication channels, from website copy to social media posts.
- **Design Your Visual Assets:** Create a logo, color palette, and website design that visually represents your brand identity.
- **Craft Your Brand Story Narrative:** Weave your brand story into your content marketing strategy, showcasing your values and mission in action.

Remember: Your brand identity is a living entity that evolves over time. As your business grows and your audience matures, revisit your brand story and messaging to

ensure it continues to resonate and effectively represent your online presence.

Content Creation Essentials: Attracting Your Target Audience with Valuable Content

You've identified your niche, chosen your business model, and crafted a brand identity that resonates with your ideal audience. Now, it's time to establish yourself as a thought leader within your niche by creating high-quality, valuable content that attracts, engages, and converts your target audience.

Content is King (or Queen) in the Online World

In today's information age, content reigns supreme. It's the cornerstone of your online presence, attracting visitors, building trust, and ultimately driving sales or client acquisition. Here's why content creation is essential for your online business:

- **Establishes You as an Authority:** By consistently creating informative and insightful content, you position yourself as a trusted expert within your niche.
- **Attracts Your Ideal Audience:** Targeted content that addresses your audience's needs and interests draws them to your website or online platform.
- **Builds Relationships and Trust:** Valuable content fosters trust and encourages audience engagement, creating a foundation for long-term relationships.
- **Drives Conversions:** Informative content educates your audience about your offerings, ultimately leading them toward becoming paying customers or clients.

Content Creation Essentials:

Here are the key elements to consider when crafting valuable content:

- **Know Your Audience:** Tailor your content to the specific needs, challenges, and preferred learning styles of your target audience.

- **Focus on Value:** Every piece of content you create should offer something valuable to your audience, whether it's solving a problem, providing new information, or inspiring them to take action.
- **Content Variety:** Experiment with different content formats like blog posts, infographics, videos, podcasts, or even webinars to cater to diverse learning preferences.
- **Consistency is Key:** Develop a consistent content creation schedule to keep your audience engaged and coming back for more.

Content Brainstorming and Planning:

To ensure your content creation efforts are strategic and effective, follow these steps:

- **Conduct Keyword Research:** Determine which terms your target audience employs when searching for information online.
- **Analyze Industry Trends:** Stay up-to-date on current trends and discussions within your niche to inform your content calendar.

- **Content Calendar Creation:** Develop a content calendar that outlines your content ideas, formats, and publishing schedule.

Optimizing Your Content for Search Engines (SEO):

While creating valuable content is crucial, ensuring it's discoverable is equally important. Here are some basic SEO (Search Engine Optimization) practices to consider:

- **Keyword Integration:** Strategically integrate relevant keywords throughout your content, but prioritize readability over keyword stuffing.
- **Meta Descriptions and Titles:** Craft compelling meta descriptions and titles that accurately reflect your content and entice clicks in search results.
- **Internal Linking:** Link your new content to relevant existing content on your website to improve user experience and search engine ranking.

Remember: Content creation is an ongoing process. Analyze your content performance, track audience engagement metrics, and adapt your strategy to continuously improve the value and reach of your online presence.

CHAPTER 7:

LAUNCHING AND GROWING YOUR ONLINE BUSINESS: ESSENTIAL TOOLS AND STRATEGIES

Building Your Digital Home: Essential Website Creation Platforms

Now that you've established your brand identity and honed your content creation skills, it's time to construct the foundation of your online presence – your website. Here, we'll explore some popular website creation platforms to get you started:

. **Website Builders (Wix, Squarespace):** Ideal for beginners with user-friendly interfaces and drag-and-drop functionality. Offer pre-designed templates and built-in features like contact forms and galleries.

. **Content Management Systems (CMS) (WordPress, Joomla):** Provide greater flexibility and customization options. Requires more technical knowledge but offers extensive plugin support and scalability for future growth.

. **E-commerce Platforms (Shopify, BigCommerce):** Designed specifically for online stores, offering shopping cart functionality, product management tools, and secure payment gateways.

Choosing the Right Platform:

Consider these factors when selecting your website creation platform:

. **Technical Expertise:** How comfortable are you with website development?

. **Scalability Needs:** Do you anticipate your website growing significantly in the future?

. **Budget:** Website builders often have monthly fees, while CMS platforms might require additional costs for themes and plugins.

- **Features and Functionality:** Ensure the platform offers the features you need, such as contact forms, e-commerce functionality, or appointment scheduling.

Beyond the Platform:

Remember, your website creation platform is just one piece of the puzzle. Here are additional considerations:

- **Domain Name:** Choose a memorable and brand-aligned domain name that reflects your niche and business identity.
- **Web Hosting:** Select a reliable web hosting provider to ensure your website is accessible to visitors 24/7.
- **Website Design:** Invest in a professional website design that is visually appealing, user-friendly, and optimized for mobile devices.

Spreading the Word: Effective Marketing Tactics for Online Businesses

With your website up and running, it's time to attract visitors and convert them into paying customers or loyal fans. Here are some excellent marketing strategies to consider:

- **Search Engine Optimization (SEO):** Implement SEO best practices to improve your website's ranking in search engine results pages (SERPs) for relevant keywords.
- **Content Marketing:** Consistently create valuable content that educates, entertains, or inspires your target audience, driving traffic to your website and establishing you as a thought leader.
- **Social Media Marketing:** Engage with your audience on relevant social media platforms, share valuable content, and participate in industry conversations.

- **Email Marketing:** Build an email list and nurture leads with targeted email campaigns that promote your content, offerings, and special promotions.
- **Paid Advertising:** Consider paid advertising platforms like Google Ads or social media advertising to reach a wider audience and target specific demographics.

Remember: The most effective marketing strategies often combine these tactics. Experiment, track your results, and refine your approach to maximize your return on investment (ROI).

Content is King (and Queen): Strategies to Leverage Different Formats

We previously established content as the cornerstone of your online presence. Now, let's delve into strategies for leveraging different content formats to maximize your reach and impact:

- **Blog Posts:** Establish yourself as an authority with informative and engaging blog posts that address your audience's needs and pain points.
- **Infographics:** Display complex information in a visually appealing and easily accessible manner.
- **Videos:** Engage your audience with video tutorials, interviews with industry experts, or behind-the-scenes glimpses into your business.
- **Podcasts:** Reach an audience on the go with informative or entertaining podcasts related to your niche.
- **Webinars:** Host live or pre-recorded webinars to provide in-depth information and establish yourself as an expert.
- **Ebooks and Lead Magnets:** Offer valuable downloadable content like ebooks or white papers in exchange for email addresses, building your email list, and nurturing leads.

Reaching a Wider Audience:

- **Guest Blogging:** Contribute guest posts to relevant websites or blogs within your niche to reach a wider audience and establish backlinks to your own website (SEO benefit).
- **Social Media Content Sharing:** Tailor your content to different social media platforms, leveraging visuals and engaging captions to encourage sharing.
- **Collaborations:** Partner with other influencers or businesses within your niche for collaborative content creation or joint promotions.

Remember: Consistency is key. Develop a content calendar that incorporates various formats and publish content regularly to keep your audience engaged and coming back for more.

By leveraging the website creation platforms, effective marketing tactics,

CONCLUSION:

THE NICHE MASTERY JOURNEY - A LIFELONG PURSUIT OF SUCCESS

Continuous Learning and Niche Refinement

Congratulations! You've embarked on the exciting journey of navigating your niche and building a thriving online business. This journey is not a sprint; it's a lifelong pursuit of growth, learning, and adaptation. Here are some key takeaways to remember as you venture forward:

. **Embrace the Power of Niche:** A well-defined niche allows you to become a recognized authority, cultivate a loyal audience, and ultimately build a sustainable business.

. **Lifelong Learning is Essential:** The online landscape is constantly evolving. Stay curious, keep learning about your niche and industry trends, and adapt your strategies accordingly.

. **Experimentation is Your Friend:** Don't be afraid to experiment with different content formats, marketing tactics, and business models. Analyze your results, learn from your experiences, and refine your approach.

. **Community is Key:** Building relationships with other niche enthusiasts, collaborators, and even competitors can foster learning, support, and shared success.

. **Passion is Your Fuel:** Building a successful online business requires dedication and perseverance. Let your passion for your niche fuel your journey and keep you motivated through challenges.

The Road Ahead

The chapters within this guide have equipped you with the foundational knowledge and practical strategies to launch and grow your online business. Remember, success doesn't happen overnight. Be patient, celebrate your milestones, and continuously strive to add value to your audience. As you navigate the ever-evolving online world, embrace the challenges, celebrate the victories, and enjoy the lifelong pursuit of building something meaningful within your chosen niche.

The Adventure Continues:

The world of online business is large and constantly changing. There's always more to learn and explore. Continue your learning journey by:

- **Reading Industry Publications:** Stay up-to-date on the latest trends and best practices by subscribing to industry publications and blogs.
- **Attending Online Courses and Workshops:** Invest in your knowledge by enrolling in online courses or attending workshops specific to your niche or business needs.
- **Connecting with Mentors and Coaches:** Seek guidance from experienced mentors or coaches who can offer valuable insights and support throughout your entrepreneurial journey.

Remember, the most successful Niche Masterys are those who never stop learning, adapting, and growing. With dedication, passion, and the knowledge you've gained, you're well-equipped to carve your unique path to online business success. Now, go forth and conquer your niche!

<u>Embracing Growth and Adaptation</u>

Congratulations! You've embarked on the dynamic voyage of the Niche Mastery. This isn't a journey with a fixed destination; it's a continuous exploration of learning, refinement, and adaptation. As you navigate the ever-evolving online landscape, remember these essential principles:

- **The Niche is a Living Ecosystem:** Your niche isn't static. Trends shift, audiences evolve, and competitor strategies change. Embrace continuous learning to stay ahead of the curve and adjust your approach accordingly.

. **Refine, Don't Abandon:** As you learn and grow, your niche focus might naturally refine. Don't be afraid to niche down further or adjust your offerings to better serve your ideal audience's needs.

. **Embrace Experimentation:** Treat your online business as a playground for experimentation. Test new content formats, marketing tactics, and business models. Data and audience feedback will guide you towards what resonates most.

. **Growth is a Mindset:** Don't be afraid to step outside your comfort zone. Accept obstacles as opportunities to learn and improve. Celebrate your successes, big and small, and keep pushing yourself to expand your knowledge and expertise.

. **The Power of Community:** Collaboration is key. Connect with other niche enthusiasts, industry leaders, and even supportive competitors. Sharing ideas, fostering partnerships, and learning from diverse perspectives fuels innovation and growth.

The Continuous Learning Loop

The chapters within this guide have equipped you with the foundational tools to navigate your niche. However, the learning journey never ends. Here's how you remain at the forefront:

. **Become a Voracious Learner:** Devour industry publications, blogs, and online courses related to your niche and broader online business trends.
. **Seek Mentorship and Coaching:** Invest in your growth by seeking guidance from experienced mentors or coaches who can offer valuable insights and support.
. **Engage with Your Audience:** Actively listen to your audience's needs and feedback. Conduct surveys, analyze website data, and participate in industry forums to understand their evolving interests and pain points.

Growth and Adaptation: The Hallmarks of Success

The most successful Niche Masterys are lifelong learners who adapt to change. By embracing continuous learning, refining your niche focus strategically, and fostering a growth mindset, you'll be well-equipped to navigate the ever-changing online landscape. Remember that the journey is as essential as the destination. Remember that the journey is as essential as the destination. So, enjoy the process, celebrate your progress, and keep exploring the exciting possibilities within your niche.

The Unfolding Adventure Awaits:

As you venture forth, remember that the online world offers endless opportunities for growth and exploration. Here are some more recommendations to fuel your journey:

- **Attend Industry Events:** Network with other entrepreneurs, learn from leading experts and discover cutting-edge trends by attending industry conferences, workshops, or online webinars.

- **Contribute to the Community:** Share your expertise by guest blogging, participating in online forums, or even creating your own educational content to give back to the community that has helped you grow.
- **Embrace New Technologies:** Stay informed about emerging technologies that could impact your niche or business operations. Be open to exploring new tools and platforms to enhance your offerings and streamline your processes.

The world of online business is a dynamic ecosystem, and you are the captain of your own ship. With a thirst for knowledge, a willingness to adapt, and a commitment to growth, you'll be well on your way to carving your unique path to success within your chosen niche. Bon voyage, Niche Mastery!

The Power of Community - Building Networks and Sharing Your Entrepreneurial Journey

*C*ongratulations! You've embarked on the exhilarating journey of the Niche Mastery. This path isn't a solitary trek; it thrives on the power of connection and shared experiences. As you navigate the exciting yet challenging world of online business, remember the invaluable role the community plays in your success.

Building Your Support System:

The online landscape can feel vast and overwhelming at times. Here's how fostering a strong community can empower your entrepreneurial journey:

. **Collaboration is Key:** Connect with other niche enthusiasts, industry leaders, and even supportive competitors. Sharing ideas, brainstorming solutions, and fostering partnerships can spark innovation and accelerate your growth.

. **Peer-to-Peer Learning:** Engage with online forums, mastermind groups, or niche-specific social media communities. Learn from the experiences of others, share your own challenges, and benefit from diverse perspectives.

. **Mentorship and Coaching:** Seek guidance from experienced mentors or coaches who can offer valuable insights, support your decision-making, and hold you accountable for your goals.

The Power of Shared Experiences:

Your entrepreneurial journey is a rich tapestry woven with triumphs and challenges. Building a community allows you to:

. **Celebrate Milestones:** Share your successes, big and small, with your community. Their encouragement and recognition will fuel your motivation and keep you moving forward.

- **Seek Support During Challenges:** Inevitably, you'll encounter roadblocks. A supportive community provides a safe space to voice your concerns, receive constructive feedback, and find solutions collaboratively.
- **Inspire and Be Inspired:** Share your knowledge and expertise with others. Witnessing the impact you make on others will strengthen your resolve and fuel your passion for your niche.

Building Bridges Within Your Niche:

Here are some actionable steps to actively build your niche community:

- **Engage on Social Media:** Join relevant Facebook groups, participate in Twitter chats, and connect with other niche influencers on various platforms. Share valuable content, engage in meaningful discussions, and build genuine relationships.

- **Host Online Events:** Organize webinars, workshops, or online Q&A sessions to share your expertise and connect with your audience on a deeper level.

- **Contribute to the Conversation:** Guest blog for other niche websites, participate in industry podcasts, or even start your own blog or online forum to share your knowledge and contribute to the collective understanding of your niche.

The Journey is a Shared Experience

The road to online business success is paved with connections and shared experiences. By fostering a strong community around your niche, you not only gain invaluable support but also contribute to the collective knowledge and growth of your chosen field. Remember, **"together we rise"!** As you venture forth on your Niche Mastery journey, embrace the power of community, build bridges of collaboration, and share your story to inspire others.

The Adventure Continues:

The online world pulsates with the energy of vibrant communities. Here are some additional ways to leverage the power of connection:

- **Become a Mentor:** As you gain experience, pay it forward by offering mentorship or coaching to aspiring Niche Masterys.
- **Advocate for Collaboration:** Promote the importance of collaboration within your niche. Encourage others to connect, share resources, and support each other's growth.
- **Celebrate Community Wins:** Recognize and celebrate the successes of others within your community. This fosters a spirit of camaraderie and motivates everyone to strive for excellence.

By actively building and engaging within your niche community, you'll not only enrich your own entrepreneurial journey but also contribute to a thriving ecosystem of shared knowledge, support, and innovation. Bon voyage, Niche Mastery, and may your journey be filled with the power of connection!

Your First Steps Towards Online Business Success

Congratulations! You've embarked on the exciting yet challenging journey of the Niche Mastery. This guide has equipped you with the knowledge and tools to navigate your chosen niche and build a thriving online business. However, knowledge without action is like a treasure chest buried deep – its potential remains unfulfilled.

The Power of the First Step

The road to online business success begins with a single, decisive action. Here's why taking action is crucial:

- **Breaking the Inertia:** Overcoming that initial hurdle of inaction is often the toughest part. Taking the first step builds momentum and propels you forward on your entrepreneurial journey.

- **Learning Through Doing:** While knowledge is essential, true understanding comes from experience. Taking action allows you to test your ideas, learn from mistakes, and refine your approach.
- **Building Confidence:** Each completed task, and each milestone achieved, fuels your confidence and validates your ability to succeed.

Taking Action: A Practical Roadmap

Here's a practical roadmap to get you started on your online business journey:

- **Refine Your Niche:** Based on the knowledge gained, revisit your niche selection. Consider refining your focus to cater to a more specific audience.
- **Choose Your Business Model:** Select the business model that aligns with your niche, interests, and long-term goals (e.g., affiliate marketing, e-commerce, coaching).
- **Craft Your Brand Identity:** Develop a clear brand story, define your brand voice and personality, and create visual elements (logo,

color scheme) that resonate with your target audience.

- **Build Your Digital Home:** Choose a website creation platform that suits your skills and budget. Develop a user-friendly and visually appealing website that reflects your brand identity.
- **Content is King (and Queen):** Develop a content calendar and start creating valuable content that educates, entertains, or inspires your target audience.

Remember: This is just the beginning. Don't get overwhelmed by the enormity of the task. Focus on taking small, consistent actions each day. Celebrate your progress, no matter how small, and keep moving forward.

Embrace the Journey, Not Just the Destination

Building a successful online business takes time, dedication, and perseverance. The journey itself is filled with learning opportunities, unexpected turns, and moments of both triumph and challenge. Here's how to approach this entrepreneurial adventure:

- **Embrace the Learning Curve:** Expect to make mistakes. View them as learning opportunities, adjust your approach, and keep moving forward.
- **Celebrate Milestones:** Acknowledge and celebrate your progress, big and small. These moments of recognition will fuel your motivation and keep you going.
- **Nurture Your Passion:** Keep in mind what sparked your interest in your niche. Let your passion guide your decisions and fuel your creativity.

The Adventure Awaits

The online world offers a boundless landscape of possibilities for those who dare to take action. With the knowledge you've gained, a thirst for learning, and the unwavering spirit of a Niche Mastery, you're well-equipped to carve your own path to success. Now, go forth, take that first step, and watch your online business dreams take flight!

Bonus Tip: Share your journey with others! Document your progress, challenges, and successes on a blog or social media platform. This not only fosters accountability but also inspires others to embark on their own entrepreneurial adventures.

Profitable Niches for Beginners: Launching Quickly and Leveraging Your Skills

The exciting world of online business offers a plethora of niches for aspiring entrepreneurs. Here are some profitable niches that beginners can consider, along with tips to leverage your existing skills and launch quickly:

1. Social Media Management:

- **Profitability:** Businesses of all sizes recognize the power of social media but lack the time or expertise to manage it effectively.
- **Leveraging Skills:** Do you have a knack for social media engagement? Can you curate visually appealing content and craft compelling captions? If so, this niche could be a perfect fit.

Quick Launch Tips:
- **Develop Sample Packages:** Create pre-defined social media management packages with clear deliverables (e.g., post creation, community engagement, reporting).
- **Offer Free Consultations:** Connect with potential clients by offering free consultations to understand their needs and showcase your expertise.
- **Utilize Social Proof:** Build trust by showcasing testimonials from satisfied clients on your website or social media profiles.

2. Virtual Assistant Services:

- **Profitability:** Busy entrepreneurs and businesses often require administrative or technical support. Virtual assistants can handle tasks like email management, scheduling, data entry, and bookkeeping remotely.
- **Leveraging Skills:** Are you organized, detail-oriented, and possess strong communication skills? These are valuable assets for virtual assistant services.

Quick Launch Tips:

- **Highlight Transferable Skills:** Focus on transferable skills like project management, communication, and time management in your marketing materials.
- **Offer Niche-Specific Packages:** Consider specializing in a particular industry (e.g., e-commerce, real estate) to attract targeted clientele.
- **Network with Freelancing Platforms:** Sign up on popular freelancing platforms

like Upwork or Fiverr to connect with potential clients.

3. Content Creation (Blogging, Writing, Video Editing):

- Profitability: Businesses and individuals require engaging content for their websites, social media platforms, and marketing campaigns.
- Leveraging Skills: Do you enjoy writing, have a creative flair for video editing, or possess a knack for storytelling? These skills are valuable in the content creation niche.

Quick Launch Tips:

- **Build a Content Portfolio:** Create a website or online portfolio showcasing your best writing samples, video editing skills, or blog posts.
- **Guest Blogging:** Reach a wider audience and establish yourself as an expert by guest blogging on relevant websites within your chosen niche.

- **Offer Content Packages:** Develop content creation packages that cater to specific client needs (e.g., blog post creation, social media content calendar, video editing).

4. **Online Fitness Coaching:**
   - **Profitability:** The health and wellness industry is booming, and people are increasingly seeking online fitness coaching for personalized guidance and flexibility.
   - **Leveraging Skills:** Are you a certified fitness professional passionate about helping others achieve their fitness goals? If so, this niche offers a rewarding opportunity.

Quick Launch Tips:
- **Offer Free Consultations:** Connect with potential clients by offering free consultations to assess their fitness levels and discuss their goals.

- **Utilize Online Platforms:** Leverage online fitness platforms like Zoom or Teachable to deliver personalized coaching sessions and workout plans.
- **Build a Social Media Community:** Share fitness tips, healthy recipes, and motivational content on social media to attract potential clients and build a strong online presence.

REMEMBER:

- **Passion is key:** Choose a niche that you are actually interested in. Your enthusiasm will translate into engaging content, effective service delivery, and ultimately, a successful online business.
- **Focus on Value:** Always provide exceptional value to your clients or audience. This could be through informative content, personalized services, or high-quality products.
- **Continuous Learning:** The online landscape is constantly evolving. Stay updated with industry trends and invest in

acquiring new skills to remain competitive.

GOOD LUCK AS YOU JOURNEY THROUGH THE WORLD OF MARKETING AND CONQUERING THE DIGITAL WORLD AND I WISH YOU SUCCESS IN YOUR JOURNEY AS YOU EXPLORE YOUR DIFFERENT NICHES.

Coulter J. Weldon

---

www.ingramcontent.com/pod-product-compliance
Lightning Source LLC
Chambersburg PA
CBHW050107230526
45470CB00004B/1722